BLUFF YOUR WAY IN THE EUROPEAN UNION

MICHAEL TONER & CHRISTOPHER WHITE

D1144376

RAVETTE PUBLISHING

Published by Ravette Publishing Limited
P.O. Box 296
Horsham
West Sussex RH13 8FH
Telephone: (01403) 711443
Fax: (01403) 711554

First printed 1988, updated 1991
New edition 1992, reprinted 1993
New edition 1995, reprinted 1996

Series Editor – Anne Tauté

Cover design – Jim Wire
Printing & Binding – Cox & Wyman Ltd.
Production – Oval Projects Ltd.

The Bluffer's Guides® series is based
on an original idea by Peter Wolfe.

An **Oval Project**
for Ravette Publishing.

Cover: Flags of some EU Nations
(*from left to right*)
Germany; Ireland; Netherlands;
Denmark; Portugal; Britain;
Belgium; Greece; Spain;
Luxembourg; Italy; France.

CONTENTS

INTRODUCTION

The European Union offers the ideal opportunity for some serious bluffing. You can climb every mountain, ford every stream, but in all your travels you will seldom meet anyone who has a clue how it got started, how it works, or who isn't secretly worried about where it is going.

There are, it is true, a few politicians, bureaucrats and Eurofanatics who are quite at home discussing Subsidiarity or the benefits of the Lomé Convention. Such people tend to describe themselves as Federalists and are instantly recognisable by their fixed grins and staring eyes. Luckily they are so incredibly boring that they are seldom invited out in civilised company.

This leaves the field clear for the bluffer to hold forth without serious risk of challenge. Some Members of the European Parliament have built their entire careers upon this happy basis.

The first rule for the serious bluffer is to refer to this extraordinary institution by its correct title. You certainly will not have the bad taste to refer to it as 'The EEC' or even 'The EC'. Such solecisms will mark you out as an amateur, even if you are able to recite Schiller's *Ode to Joy* from memory, or know all the Kings of France or understand the origins of the Thirty Years War.

You will know that the outfit which started life as 'The Common Market' was known officially as The European Economic Community until the passage (in 1987) of the Single European Act, when it became simply the European Community or EC. But that, with the advent of the Maastricht Treaties, the plain old EC was transformed into something much grander, The European Union, or EU.

5

By all means refer to the European Union, since it's the convenient thing to do. But do not be shy about throwing in the odd reference to the European Community. When eyebrows are raised, you may loftily point out that strictly speaking, references to the EU should only apply to meetings of the Council of Ministers. This is a fine, legalistic quibble and should win you no end of esteem.

But if ever you are confronted by someone who insists on referring to 'The Union' in tones of hushed piety, have a care. This will be a True Believer, and is best handled gently. Smile genially as he or she expounds upon Europe's civilising mission. Nod sagely at the claim that the term 'Union' faithfully reflects the way so many nation states are working selflessly together. On no account mention the last disastrous political alliance which laid claim to the word: the Soviet Union.

THE BASICS

Without being fanatical, a determined Euro-bluffer should try to applaud and uphold the EU at all times. Never mind if you think the institution is a joke in poor taste. Or if you actually voted against joining. No-one will ever know.

Tell yourself firmly that the mere existence of the EU constitutes "The most remarkable collaborative political venture of our century". If you repeat this mantra several times each night before going to sleep you will certainly convince yourself. And in time you will gain the reputation of being a true European.

"That's all very well," someone is bound to say, "But we're losing our identity, aren't we? We're being herded into an economic and monetary union. We're being dragooned into a European superstate. And nobody's bothering to ask our opinion."

Rather than get into discussing facts – a good bluffer must never let the facts get in the way of winning an argument – you will stress, again and with great meaning, the word 'venture'. Except this time, call it a 'brave venture'. Point out that the fruits lie in the future, that we should all look to the future, not the past or even the present, that sacrifices, if any, are made for our children's sake and for generations as yet unborn.

Do not, for one moment, think that your listeners will rise up as one and strike you to the ground when you come out with such palpable clap-trap. The same nonsense has been used by various communist states, town planners and England's football selectors for years. And they invariably get away with it.

Members

In any discussion about the EU, some smart-alec is bound to challenge you to name all the member countries. Any bluffer worth his salt will rattle them off without a moment's hesitation:

Austria	France	Luxembourg
Belgium	Germany	Netherlands
Britain	Greece	Portugal
Denmark	Ireland	Spain
Finland	Italy	Sweden

At this point you should adopt a knowing expression and murmur that of course the Union is bound to grow bigger. 'Enlargement' is the word to use. It will establish your expertise beyond question. Never mind the fact that the Norwegians, in a fit of good old Norse independence, turned down the opportunity to sign up, (this is so often the trouble with a referendum: it allows ordinary folk to throw their weight around). Many nations of the old Soviet empire, particularly Hungary, Poland, the Czech Republic and Slovakia are sniffing at the Union's gates*, as are Cyprus and Malta.

Boldly assert that the whole point of the Union is that it manages to accommodate the differences between member states: they differ in language, religion, outlook and economic performance but manage to co-operate just the same. And never neglect an opportunity to point out the near-miraculous achievement of the European Union in persuading such a bunch of suspicious, antagonistic and aggressive nations to work together.

*Morroco's ambition to join is nowadays a bit of a dead duck. This doesn't matter since most Morrocans are already living in France and Belgium.

It will help if you have at your command a few well-honed aphorisms about the member states. You might, for example, assert that:

– the British are still shell-shocked by the loss of Empire, and only joined because they thought they could run Europe instead.

– the French were prime instigators of the EC because they got fed up with being invaded so regularly by the Germans, who kept drinking their wine and taking their women without so much as a by your leave.

– the Belgians are in because they got fed up with the Germans marching through on their way to beat the French. And hardly bothered to cast an eye at their women, let alone their wine.

– the Germans joined because it gave them a chance to dominate when invasion became unfashionable.

– the Danes joined in an attempt to live down the Vikings who went in for a lot of rape and pillage; and they needed to secure a market for their bacon.

– the Irish prefer Guinness to wine or women. They only joined because they were convinced that those cunning blackguards in Britain must know something that they didn't.

– the Italians, Spanish and Portuguese all joined because they could not bear to be left out.

– the Greeks are members in order to dish the Turks.

– the Dutch joined because they are a decent, warm-hearted people who care deeply about the principle of European unity.

Nobody cares why Luxembourg joined.

You can also point out that most of the misunderstandings within the EU are in fact caused by its peoples being either Puritans, or those lucky souls who can enjoy themselves without guilt. Most, if not all, of the former are Protestant, while the latter tend to be Catholics with a strong pagan tradition.

For example, much of the trouble between the French and the English is caused by a French inability to understand that when young Englishmen get drunk, strip naked, wave flags and urinate in public fountains, they are really feeling guilty about wanting to enjoy themselves, since England is basically a puritanical society. The French apparently feel that there is nothing wrong with Britain's young that a few companies of riot police couldn't sort out.

Loads of People

There are 410 million people in the Union; and though these souls amount to only seven per cent of the planet's population, they matter because in world terms they are rich. Filthy rich.

Now the bluffer is bound to encounter critics who claim that this is all eyewash. They will fix you with their beady eyes and complain that unemployment in Europe is unacceptably high. The thing to do is to put on an expression which is at once sympathetic and condescending and explain that you're talking about global perspectives.

Never mind the threat from the tiger economies of Asia. You should assert that the trading power and yet untapped potential of the Union is so great that we don't have to play second fiddle to anybody. We are not only rich but we have plenty of opportunity to grow richer still. This is sometimes known as the European Ideal.

Dates To Remember

You need never be shy of claiming British authorship of the European Union. Not only will such boldness mark you out as someone to be reckoned with, but it can be guaranteed to enrage any Frenchman in the vicinity.

In September, 1946, Winston Churchill delivered a remarkable speech in Zurich calling for the establishment of "a kind of United States of Europe".

This was regarded as hot stuff at the time. Not only did it mark a major gesture of post-war reconciliation but it tapped into a growing European mood.

The French of course, like to claim that the whole thrust towards closer European integration was all their doing, despite Mr. Churchill's speech and the foundation of an economic union between Belgium, the Netherlands and Luxembourg (Benelux) in 1947. The French may have a point, but you are not obliged to take any notice of it.

It is quite unnecessary to know the minor details of who started the ball rolling or how the whole thing developed. If the discussion starts to grow heated on such questions your best bet is to purse your lips and murmur how distressing it is to hear such nationalistic bombast creeping into the discussion.

All you really need to grasp is a handful of key dates and references and you should compel the respectful attention of almost any company:

April 1951:	The Treaty of Paris sets up the European Coal and Steel Community (ECSC) with six members – Germany, France, the Netherlands, Belgium, Luxembourg and Italy.
March 1957:	The six members of the ECSC sign the Treaties of Rome, setting up the EEC and the European Atomic Energy Community (Euratom).
July/Aug. 1961:	Britain applies to join the EEC, along with Ireland and Denmark. French President, de Gaulle, says "Non".
May 1967:	Britain tries yet again, along with Ireland, Denmark and, later, Norway. But still the General will not have it.
January 1973:	The Six become The Nine. Britain, Ireland and Denmark are allowed in at last. (Norway's bid collapses when its people say "No".)
March 1979:	Creation of the European Monetary Systems (EMS). Britain chooses not to join (largely because its Treasury cannot understand the system).
June 1979:	First direct elections to European Parliament.
January 1981:	And then there were Ten. Greece joins the EEC.

June 1985:	Spain and Portugal sign the Treaty of Accession. The Ten becomes The Twelve.
February 1986:	The Single European Act is signed. The EC is set to become a genuine single market with differential tariffs and other restraints on trade removed by December 31, 1992.
February 1992:	The Treaties of European Union are signed at Maastricht with eleven members solemnly agreeing to go for full economic and monetary union and Britain agreeing only if allowed time for a re-think.
June 1992:	The Maastricht Treaties collapse when, after a national referendum, Denmark says "No".
September 1992:	Britain is driven out of the Exchange-Rate Mechanism on 'Black Wednesday', after the Germans refuse to bail out the pound.
May 1993:	The Maastricht Treaties are revived when the Danes are bribed and bullied into changing their minds.
January 1995:	Austria, Finland and Sweden join. The Twelve become the Fifteen.
1996:	An inter-governmental conference is forecast, when the plan is to bribe and bully everyone else into going even further down the road to European integration.

INSTITUTIONS OF THE EU

Sooner or later the Euro-bluffer will have to come to grips with a group of people whose reputation inspires universal terror and detestation. We are not referring to English football hooligans or German tourists, but those strange, half-mythical beings known collectively as The Faceless Bureaucrats of Brussels.

You can always tell when the Faceless Ones have been at work. Their efforts make marvellous headlines:

- Britain must Drive on the Right says Brussels

- Change Name of Waterloo Station Demands EU – It's an 'Insult' to the French

- Brussels Bans abnormal curves in Bananas

- London's Double-Decker Buses Must Go, says EU

Whether or not such tales bear much relation to the truth they are certain to crop up in any discussion of the EU, and unless you are mighty careful you may find the initiative slipping away from you. The trouble is, there are so many foolish ideas floating around Brussels that every Tom, Dick and Harry feels entitled to sound off about them.

This will never do. Once the talk turns to the latest example of Euro lunacy, you must nip it in the bud at once. Otherwise you may never get a word in.

Shake your head thoughtfully and assert that the issue under debate, let's say the harmonisation of sausages, is not as simple as all that. "It'll never get through at Strasbourg" you might say. Or: "I can't see the Council of Ministers wearing it."

Real experts have it off pat. They'll curl a lip, assume a lofty expression and explain condescendingly that each and every example of barminess from Brussels has been made up by the press.

Copy their example. Practice in front of a mirror until you've mastered that special look of disdain. Scoff at all those reports of supposed 'bans' on mushy peas, saucy seaside postcards and youngsters doing the paper round. Have any such bans been put into practice? Of course not. No wonder Europe is so unpopular when rapscallion reporters can't be trusted to get it right.

But do be careful. One of your listeners may be a reporter. Or a reasonably well-informed Euro-sceptic. In which case you should move smoothly to Plan 2.

This also involves a curl of the lip and a lofty expression. Only this time the target of your ire has changed. Say that the Faceless Ones have indeed laid down strict regulations about bananas – a minimum of 5.5 inches long and 1.06 inches round, to be exact. What is more, despite claims to cut down on mad bureaucracy, the number of EU Directives and Regulations in 1994 shot up from 1,602 to 1,800.

With any luck, this should silence the entire company leaving you free to state that with the way Europe is run by five key institutions – the Commission, the Council of Ministers, the European Parliament, the European Court of Justice and the Court of Auditors – it's a minor miracle any decisions get taken at all.

The Commission

The boast of the European Commission is that it is the engine-room of of the Union. However you can wander all day round the depressingly ugly Breydel building in Brussels – headquarters of the Commission – and never see anybody who looks remotely like a stoker.

What you will see are hordes of nattily-dressed, important-looking bureaucrats who all seem inordinately pleased with themselves. No wonder. The Commission not only administers the day-to-day running of the Union, it also proposes new policies, drafts legislation for the European Parliament and acts as Guardian of the Treaties.

Never be taken in by the claim that the EU is run by democratically-elected politicians. Any government which fails to toe the line is liable to be hauled before the European Court and ordered to mend its ways. The moral is that none of them should have joined if they couldn't take a joke.

At the head of this bureaucratic powerhouse of 13,000 civil servants are seventeen Commissioners, who are appointed by the national governments. The bigger countries – Britain, France, Germany, Italy and Spain have the right to nominate two Commissioners each. The others appoint only one.

Whatever you do, avoid the trap of assuming that because the Commissioners are appointed by their home governments they are subject to political control. Nothing of the kind. The independence of the Commissioners is guaranteed by:

The Oath

Before anybody can become a Commissioner he must swear a mighty Oath that he will be faithful to the European Union alone, and serve only the Union, regardless of what his Government back home might think, his own personal preferences, or common sense.

If he forswears this solemn obligation, may his heart

be ripped out by the vultures, may he be buried to the neck by the waterline at low tide, may his expense claims become public.

You should never underestimate the power of this Oath. Most Commissioners take it so seriously that they are frequently accused in their home countries of near-treasonable behaviour. However, with their plush offices, their huge staffs, their cars, expenses and vast, tax-free salaries (as near as makes no difference), they can afford to suffer the jibes of a jealous public.

In the political life of Europe, becoming a Commissioner is a splendid consolation prize for never quite having made the grade back home. It is the ultimate bluff.

The European Parliament

In order to bluff about the European Parliament you must be familiar with two propositions:

1. It's a powerless farce. A toothless tiger. Its membership is made up of failed politicians who fell short of requirements in their own national assemblies and who have been pensioned off to the fat salaries and huge expense-accounts of Strasbourg. Their deliberations are so tedious and meaningless that few newspapers ever bother to report them.

2. It's the cradle of a new democratic order which is becoming increasingly important as the EU develops. Its Members are directly elected by universal suffrage and therefore have a legitimacy which no amount of criticism can undermine. The Parliament has significant powers: it can, and sometimes does

throw out the annual budget of the Community. It can sack the entire Commission if it feels so inclined. It scrutinises and often changes proposed legislation.

It is perfectly in order to embrace both of these apparently contradictory views (though not necessarily at the same time).

What you should point out is that events in Europe are developing so fast that it is impossible to be dogmatic about the Parliament. With the ratification of the Maastricht Treaties, MEPs won new powers to influence the way the EU is run, including the right to veto the appointment of new Commissioners. For the first time, the Strasbourg Parliament might be worth taking seriously, though whether MEPs are capable of seizing their new opportunities remains to be seen.

But by all means feel free to jeer at the shambolic way the Parliament conducts its business.

Once a month it meets for a five-day general session in the Palais de l'Europe. This is not a dance-hall, but a building of quite outstanding ugliness in Strasbourg. Members spend the rest of their time in their offices located in Brussels and Luxembourg (always assuming they can find them).

So every month, MEPs and officials pack up their files in great metal boxes called canteens and trek solemnly back and forth across the roads and skies of Europe. This madness is very good news for the airlines and road haulage companies. Nobody cares what the hapless European taxpayer thinks about it all.

Try and resist the temptation to argue that such absurdity demonstrates beyond doubt that MEPs are not fit to be left in charge of a whelk stall.

The Council of Ministers

The experienced Euro-bluffer will recognise the scene instantly. It is dawn in Brussels. A group of bleary, unshaven, bad-tempered men emerge from a meeting which has been going on all night and immediately begin hurling diplomatic insults at each other in front of the television cameras. Another session of the Council of Ministers has ended.

The great thing about the Council is that it is entirely free of idealism about the greater good of the Community. Every Minister who attends is there to grab what he can for his own country, and be damned to the rest. It is a point worth remembering when you are confronted with the claim that national governments can easily be pushed around by the EU.

To be sure, the bureaucrats in the Commission are liable to come up with daft ideas. They have enormous power over the day-to-day running of the EU. But though they can and do make major new proposals it is the Council which decides whether those proposals should go forward.

Every member state has one seat at the Council table. Usually the various Foreign Ministers attend, but if the meeting is to be devoted to a particular topic – agriculture say, or transport – then Ministers with those responsibilities will turn up instead.

In theory the Council of Ministers tries to reach its decisions unanimously. In practice it is difficult to get them all to agree on the time of day.

This can, of course, be deuced awkward. So nowadays the Council increasingly operates on system known as Qualified Majority Voting, or QMV, under which the big countries have more votes than the tiddlers. Bluffers should never neglect an opportunity to drop the initials QMV into the conversation, preferably accompanied by a slight sneer. It should not have escaped your attention that Britain's voting strength under QMV has recently been watered down.

In theory, any country claiming that a vital national interest is at stake can exercise a veto. This explains why meetings of the Council tend to drag on and on until the Ministers present are too dozy to care what they are voting for. However it should be noted that such vetoes provoke much resentment and cannot be used lightly.

There are only two other things you need to know about the Council:

1. Twice a year the heads of each national government attend, and the Council of Ministers takes on an even grander status as the European Council.

2. Each member state takes over the chair or the 'presidency' of the Council for six months, in alphabetical order. This enables small nations like Greece and Portugal to demonstrate that they can botch things up just as effectively as the big boys.

The European Court

The main thing you need to understand about the European Court of Justice is that it has nothing whatsoever to do with justice.

Its main job is to interpret the various Treaties and agreements within the EC – yes, it is correct to refer to the EC in this context – paying special attention to every last dot, comma and codicil.

Never mind if European law turns out to be onerous or

perverse in particular circumstances. The thirteen judges sitting in Luxembourg will firmly apply the letter of the law. The only consolation for the members of the EU, all of whom are regularly hauled before the Court for one infraction or another, is that it's the same for everybody.

Like most other European functionaries, the judges of the Court tend to be somewhat second division. They also conduct much of their work in Latin. This deeply humiliates the Italians, who are always being asked to translate by other nationalities, and cannot; the French, who are again reminded that France used to be an Italian province; and the English who see it all as a Popish plot. The Germans, however, like Latin. It allows them to point out, yet again, how much more logical their own language is.

The Court of Auditors

Once upon a time, bluffers could get away with treating the Luxembourg-based Court as an irrelevance. No longer.

In former days this body produced an annual report on the waste and incompetence of Brussels. Everybody read it. Everybody solemnly agreed that something must be done. Then they went off to lunch and forgot about it.

Now that has all changed. In theory at least. Under the Maastricht Treaties, the Court of Auditors has become an official institution of the EU. It no longer has to ask politely if it can see relevant documents. These days it can demand them. Or else.

This sounds like good news for everyone concerned

about fraud in the EU. But the real bluffer will not seem too impressed. Fraud is just about the fastest-growing business in Europe.

The Committee of the Regions

Not normally counted as one of the five key institutions, the Committee was set up as part of the Maastricht drive towards ever-greater political union. In theory, it is supposed to share responsibility for regional issues with the European Parliament.

Bluffers would be well advised to sniff disdainfully whenever the Committee is mentioned. City Councillors from Britain sit down on apparent terms of equality with City majors and Prime Ministers of the powerful German Lander. The result is a grotesque mismatch of political experience and expertise.

You should however, resist the temptation to describe the Committee as the most useless body in Europe. That title properly belongs to the quite separate Economic and Social Committee, which has been functioning since 1958 to no discernable purpose.

Members of this outfit are nominated by employers' organisations, trades unions and special interest groups. Their job is to advise and assist the Commission, which, of course, takes no notice. Some people claim that this Committee performs a useful function. Needless to say, such supporters are almost entirely made up of people who have been appointed to serve on it.

THE EUROPEAN MONEY TREE

(And how to shake it)

All seasoned Euro-bluffers are aware of one great truth about the Community. It is awash with funds, loans, grants, donations, scholarships and good old-fashioned fiddles. That is why the budget tends to be in a state of perpetual crisis.

There are untold numbers of people flying hither and yon, staying at comfortable hotels and eating in the smartest restaurants without ever dreaming of putting their hands in their own pockets. You can too.

In other circumstances such behaviour might aptly be described as sponging. You must put such negative thoughts firmly at the back of your mind when dealing with the EU. Remember always that it is thoroughly 'communautaire' to live the life of Riley at other folks' expense.

Let us suppose that you fancy a week in Strasbourg during the asparagus season. Well, why not? Very jolly it is too.

What you must NOT do is pay a penny of your own money on the trip. Instead you should gather together a small, congenial group of freeloaders and give yourselves a suitable title. The European Cultural Seminar, say. Or the 1992 Club, or the Young Pioneers for a Europe without Frontiers. Any old name will do.

First set yourself up and acquire some headed notepaper from the least expensive local printer you can find. Then announce that you are anxious to study the workings of the European Parliament at first hand.

Write to the nearest office of the Parliament for advice (there's one in every EU capital). Better still, enlist the aid of your local MEP, who will be pathetically

23

grateful that you know his name.

With only a little luck you should find that the Parliament will reimburse your air fare plus the cost of your hotel room when you arrive in Strasbourg. Similar arrangements exist for those claiming an urgent need to study the Commission in Brussels or the Court in Luxembourg.

Bankers, teachers, lawyers, journalists, academics and students have all taken advantage of this opportunity for a free holiday. Indeed anybody can get a snout in the Eurotrough with a little ingenuity and a claim, however spurious, to some kind of official status.

But you must play the game. Do not make the mistake of one distinguished individual whose first action on entering the Palais de l'Europe in Strasbourg was to rush up to a uniformed messenger and demand: "Ou est la salle de la Euroloot, s'il vous plait?" Such behaviour gives a bad (though accurate) impression.

There are, to be fair, rather more worthy and serious funds run by the Union. Grants for farmers and fishermen, grants for training, help for companies in depressed areas, finance for research and for cultural projects are all available. Your nearest office of the European Commission will be happy to send you the details.

The Common Agricultural Policy

The CAP offers the biggest challenge the bluffer will ever have to face. It is expensive, unwieldy, wasteful and incapable of proper reform. But don't despair. If you play your cards right, you will discover plenty of chances to shine.

Be aware that any attempt to defend the CAP is certain to produce the devastating retort: "What about the food mountains then?"

At this point you should adopt a superior smile. In fact the vast mountains of butter, beef and cereals are not quite the problem they once were and you need not be afraid to say so. Don't be put off by disbelieving sniggers. You may confidently explain that the CAP was reformed root and branch in May 1992, under the direction of the then Agriculture Commissioner, the forceful Irishman Ray MacSharry.

Farmers are no longer paid vast fortunes to produce food nobody wants. Today they are paid vast fortunes not to grow food at all. Under the MacSharry arrangements, grain prices in theory should be reduced by 30 per cent, and the price of beef should come down by 15 per cent.

With any luck this will reduce your audience to silence. You are under no obligation to add that most of the 'savings' will probably be pocketed by Europe's retail chains and food distributors. Nor need you point out that the CAP budget of thirty eight billion pounds will probably be bloated to thirty nine billion pounds under the MacSharry scheme. And it's certainly not necessary to mention the Court of Auditors has concluded that the whole plan amounts to a bureaucratic nightmare and recipe for fraud. You don't want to confuse the issue, do you?

Of course you don't. So you shouldn't mention the other, lesser-known scandals within the CAP either. Greece is awash with raisins and figs. Floods of olive oil are being produced in Italy. In Holland they have what they delicately refer to as "our spreading problem" – millions of tons of manure which they don't know what to do with.

You must regard any discussion of European agriculture as a test of ingenuity. Any fool can condemn the CAP. Any fool frequently does. Your task as a would-be expert is to explain that there is another side to the coin (unless you are confronted by a case of genuine gung-ho Eurofanaticism*, in which case adopt the stratagem recommended in Frauds and Fiddles).

Claim that:

1. Europe's bulging food stores have helped to feed millions of people in the grip of famine. European grain was a significant factor in relieving famine in the Sudan and Ethiopia.

2. The long-term problem which has convulsed rural Europe is that millions of farmers are deserting the land for the cities. In 1960, one person in five worked the land in Western Europe. Nowadays it is about one in 15. And the process of rural depopulation is continuing.

Ask the question: "We all want to see a thriving countryside, don't we?... We all want Europe to be self-sufficient in food, and for that food to be available in the shops at stable prices."

---

* Eurofanaticism: a mental abnormality, characterised by:

   a) the belief that the EU exists for the spiritual exaltation of its member states, and
   b) the ability to prove that charging EU consumers more for their own butter than the Russians pay to import it, is all perfectly sound business.

Modern medical authorities believe that Eurofanaticism derives from a thwarted childhood coupled with an unhealthy fixation about early Christian martyrs. There is no known cure for this condition.

Point out that those were the priorities grasped by Dr. Sicco Mansholt (*q.v.*) when he inspired the CAP, which was set up under Article 39 of the Treaty of Rome. Be warned though that if you pursue these arguments too far you may start to earn the reputation of being a Eurobore. The danger signs are glazed expressions and stifled yawns in those around you.

Should this fate threaten to befall you it is perfectly all right to change tack completely with the assertion: "Of course it's equally true that the CAP has wrecked world food prices, damaged farming in Australia, provoked the possibility of a trade war with the United States, devastated whole economies in Africa and forced thousands of young girls in South-East Asia into white slavery." If that doesn't wake up your audience, nothing will.

In the unlikely event that anyone challenges such apocalyptic remarks, don't panic. You can reduce the most hardened sceptic to rubble simply by expatiating on the great tobacco fiasco.

Arguably the greatest single scandal in a CAP awash with scandal is the Community's insistence in spending tens of millions of pounds every year in subsidies to Greek and Italian tobacco-growers.

To prove that you are not an anti-smoking fanatic light up a large cigar and explain that you're not against the weed as such, but that the stuff grown by the Greeks and Italians is so filthy that it almost certainly contravenes the United Nations ban on germ and chemical warfare. Yet the subsidies are huge. Most of the farmers grow it on plots of about one hectare which are useless for producing anything else. Each farmer can earn as much as the capital value of his land every year in handouts from the Commission.

The tobacco is then dumped in the poor countries of

Africa and in the nations of the old Soviet Union. End your diatribe by pointing out that at the same time as poisoning the unwary, Europe is spending billions of pounds trying to persuade its own citizens not to smoke at all. Try not to mention the world hypocrisy though. Your audience is sure to do it for you.

Frauds and Fiddles

The trouble with all discussions about the Common Agricultural Policy is that they invariably flush the True Believers out into the open.

This may be because the manifest absurdities of the CAP threaten the very reputation of the EU. Or because the spectacular waste and inefficiency make a mockery of the European dream. Either way, if you spend any time at all denouncing wine lakes, grain mountains and all the rest of it you will sooner or later be confronted with the True Believer's Reproach.

It goes something like this: "No, of course we haven't got things right yet. It's easy enough to find fault. But nobody has yet come up with a better way of stabilising farm prices, ensuring adequate food supplies and protecting rural communities. How else can we guarantee Europe's food into the next century? How else can we prevent hard-working farmers, salt of the earth, bless them – going to the wall?"

In the world of bluffing such challenges are what sort out the men from the boys.

What you must not do is try to respond in kind. The chances are that your interlocutor knows much more than you do. Instead you should look the True Believer straight in the eye and ask in tones of acute concern:

"Aren't you disturbed by all the corruption involved?"

This one is an absolute winner. It can be guaranteed to reduce any True Believer to a state of shambling incoherence.

The uncomfortable truth which all real experts understand is that the CAP has created the biggest growth industry in Europe – fraud. With subsidies in every sector running into billions of ECUs there are untold numbers of hands dipping illicitly into the Euro-till.

Nobody really knows how much all those sticky fingers have cost the EU taxpayers. You can feel free to pluck any figure out of the air in the sure and certain knowledge that you cannot be challenged. Indeed most of the rackets have yet to be exposed because the European institutions are reluctant to enquire too closely into the extent of the jiggery-pokery. They are terrified of provoking an adverse public reaction.

Never mind. The fiddles and scams which have come to light are quite sufficient to justify the bluffer's case. Take the pork carrousel, for example.

This little scheme, which may have netted millions of pounds for the IRA, was uncovered by a sharp-eyed official at a border-crossing between Eire and Northern Ireland. Farmers were taking lorry-loads of pigs across the border, collecting an authorisation for a Brussels export subsidy, and then driving back across the border at another point, collecting an authorisation for an import rebate on the way. The tale is that many of the unfortunate pigs spent their entire lives being driven round in circles.

Then there was the great olive oil fiasco. The Commission in Brussels discovered that the olive groves of Italy were apparently producing enough oil every year to float a fleet of battleships. This was disturbing news, since vast sums were having to be spent every year to buy up the surplus oil. Unfortunately it was no easy matter to check the facts. Inspectors sent to Italy to look at the figures tended to be accosted by swarthy gentlemen and advised to catch the next plane home in the interests of their health.

Unwilling to be thwarted, the Commission decided to conduct an aerial survey of the olive groves. The idea was to count the number of trees and compare that figure with the quantity of oil said to have been produced.

The findings were suspiciously inconclusive. Some folk back in Brussels whispered among themselves that the swarthy gentlemen with bulges under their left armpits had somehow sabotaged the whole exercise.

If you happen to find yourself in Italy you would be well advised not to repeat this story. Instead you should hold forth in more general terms about phantom cargoes of meat, butter and cheese 'merry-go rounds', fake documents describing ships' cargoes as of EU origin in order to attract import or export grants, the adulteration of wine and false claims for goods sold into intervention.

Nobody will dare to contradict you. Though fraud is widespread there is so little evidence about the details that you may allow your imagination free rein. You'll be astonished how many people will accept all your claims as true. Especially if you hint that you have a Sicilian Godfather. Or own an olive grove.

A typical Eurofiddle was revealed in April 1992, when the Court of Auditors reported that two well-known French and Belgian dairy companies had milked European taxpayers out of eleven million pounds by lying about their exports of cheese.

Their scams were highly profitable. The French firm claimed export refunds worth more than three hundred thousand pounds on a shipment of cheese to Poland which was found to be unfit for consumption. The same company was also caught trying to pass off sub-standard cheese as Provolone, a product which should be made from sheep-milk and which attracts high export subsidies.

Worse, tell the tale of the shipment of cheese sent to the United States which was rejected when it was found to be full of animal hairs. The European companies took it all in their stride. They simply took it back and re-exported it to other countries, picking up over £100,000 in subsidy on the way.

The merest thought of all that hairy, horrible cheese being offered to unsuspecting shoppers will certainly shut up your most sceptical interlocutor. Some of your listeners may turn pale and leave the room.

The Common Fisheries Policy

Anybody tempted to believe that the Common Agricultural policy scraped the barrel of Euro lunacy has clearly never studied the ins and outs of the Common Fisheries Policy.

Here is a plan, conceived in all good faith, to manage fish stocks, prevent overfishing and to share out the bounty of the seas fairly between the member states of the Community.

Oh dear.

In one of the greatest cock-ups of the 20th century, the CFP has contrived simultaneously to:

a) price fish out of the reach of ordinary families
b) put scores of fishermen out of business
c) encourage more cheating than a three-card trick con-man
d) throw the management of fish stocks into a state of utter shambles.

Not so long ago, the gnarled old sea salts of Brussels slapped a ban on trawling for herring in order to conserve stocks. Today there are so many herring in the waters around Europe that there is talk of plundering their breeding grounds to cut the numbers.

You should be aware that there is undoubtedly a need for some kind of European fisheries policy. The combined fishing fleets of the EU between them add up to the biggest in the world, so it clearly makes sense to enforce some mutually beneficial rules.

The trouble is that few of those making the rules have ever gutted a herring or hauled in a net. So you need never feel inhibited about dismissing the CFP as a joke in rather poor taste.

To take but one example: in Brussels the experts have decreed that fishing boats of under 10 metres in length are not subject to the usual quotas, red-tape or regulations. The result could have been predicted by an infant: boats are being built just a smidgin under the 10 metre limit, but much wider and deeper than traditional craft.

This has caused uproar in Brussels, because the new boats are actually catching more fish than anybody imagined, and making nonsense of all those painstakingly worked-out quotas. So the boys in Brussels are now solemnly considering cutting the length limit to just 8 metres.

The stage is set for a quite startling development in

marine architecture. At the present rate of progress it is likely that European fishing vessels will be so managed and manipulated by the bureaucrats of Brussels that they will end up being wider than they are long.

The day may not be far off when whole fleets of oblong fishing boats belonging to the EU will be crabbing their way across the seas – another triumph for the European spirit.

Lomé

It is a shame that the Lomé Conventions, which add up to a genuine effort by Europe to help the helpless nations of the earth, should have become a byword for the grossest kind of junketing.

Don't ever be afraid of saying so. Except when Members of the European Parliament are around. They fume at the mere mention of the word 'junket', and so they should. The term covers extended stopovers at the world's best hotels, cuddles in whirlpool baths, extraordinary banquets and the abuse of first-class airfare allowances.

Newspapers the world over have had a whale of a time reporting such matters as:

- MEPs complaining that there was no champagne in their Third World hotel.

- A £30,000 telephone bill run up by a group of 14 MEPs on a delegation to a Pacific island.

Though all of this is perfectly fair comment, you should be aware that there is a rather more important side to the story. Twice a year, representatives of 68 poor African, Caribbean and Pacific (ACP) countries meet with the EU representatives to discuss aid and trade amounting to billions of pounds.

On the other hand you could add that by dumping its huge food surpluses on the world market and shutting out the products of the Third World, Europe is wrecking the agriculture of many of those self-same countries. In fact Europe will certainly take most of the blame if the resulting dispute degenerates into a global trade war.

GREAT NAMES

Charlemagne (742-814)

Crowned Holy Roman Emperor on Christmas Day, 800 AD, Charles, King of the Franks is often held up as the original true European by people who know nothing about history.

After smashing his way round most of the known world like a medieval football hooligan, Charlemagne did indeed establish an empire covering much of the continent. Alas it did not long survive his death. Under the Treaty of Verdun, his hard-won territories were divided into three parts and given to his heirs. The Holy Roman Empire (which as we all know was neither holy nor Roman nor an empire) did linger on after a fashion until relatively modern times, as a basically German confederation.

Nowadays the annual Charlemagne Award for outstanding contributions to European Unity continues to benefit the lucky recipients to the tune of DM 5,000.

Charles de Gaulle (1890-1970)

Without doubt the most remarkable leader France has produced this century, General de Gaulle deserves a special mention in the history of the Union. He very nearly brought the whole thing crashing down in ruins.

In 1965 the European Commission, under its then President Walter Hallstein, produced a plan to give the EEC a dramatic new impetus. The plan aimed to give the Community its 'own resources', mainly raised out of customs duties on imports into Europe. The scheme was intended to make the EEC financially autonomous and to strengthen the budgetary powers of the European Parliament. As always the General had other ideas. He loftily declared that the EEC was in a state of crisis. And for seven long months the French adopted an 'empty chair' policy, boycotting all Community activities and recalling its representative from Brussels.

The row was but one example of the General's troublemaking instincts. In 1963 he sabotaged the attempt by Britain, Ireland, Denmark and Norway to join. In 1967 he did it again – delicious revenge against the British for having had a rather better War than the French.

He also signed a Treaty of friendship and co-operation with the Germans in 1963, thereby creating a Paris-Bonn axis which remains at the heart of the Community to this day.

Bluffers should know de Gaulle's maxim, that there are three ways to go to hell: one, gambling; two, women, and three, believing experts – of which gambling is the quickest, women are the most enjoyable, but believing experts is the most certain.

Walter Hallstein (1901-1982)

Walter Hallstein was leader of the German delegation to the Schuman Plan Conference in 1950, and later became President of the European Commission, in 1958.

If Walter was not on this list, the Germans would not get a mention at all, unless you care to count Adolf Hitler as an inspiration for the European ideal (which in a horrible sort of way he was).

Bluffers should think well of Walter Hallstein who, apart from his undoubted merits, has the additional advantage of not being French.

Edward Heath (1916)

It is a cruel fallacy to suggest that Mr. Heath is the least inspiring leader Europe has produced in its entire history. People who make that claim have obviously not met Chancellor Helmut Kohl of Germany.

Never mind. Edward Heath deserves his place in the list of Eurogreats because he succeeded in getting Britain to join. This was no mean achievement given that Britain had twice failed in previous attempts, not to mention the deep-seated dislike of foreigners which inspires all true Britons.

It goes without saying that Mr. Heath is more highly regarded in France, Germany, Italy, Holland, the United States and China than he is in his own land. But then he never ran any of those.

Sicco Mansholt (1908)

Sicco Mansholt is a Dutch politician considered to be the father of the Common Agricultural Policy. Poor old Sicco. What a rotten thing to be remembered for.

Jean Monnet (1888-1979)

Jean Monnet is the grandfather of the European idea, and indeed was declared an 'Honorary Citizen of Europe' at a meeting of Heads of Government in Luxembourg, in 1976.

Monnet was the inspiration behind the Schuman Plan, which really got the whole enterprise under way. Not only that, he was responsible for the 'relaunch of Europe' in 1955, which led to the setting up of the EEC and Euratom.

The French are inordinately proud of Jean Monnet's achievements, which enable them to preen themselves about France's unique contribution to European integration. It also explains why deep down, the French see the EU as a 20th century French Empire.

Robert Schuman (1880-1963)

Robert Schuman is revered by all true Eurobuffs as the author of the Schuman Plan of 1950, out of which grew the European Coal and Steel Community – which in turn led to the creation of the EEC.

Nobody gives a hoot nowadays that he was also (rather briefly) Prime Minister of France, or that he became President of the European Assembly in Strasbourg, in 1958. His claim to fame is The Plan, and if ever you hear anybody mentioning it, you will know for certain that you are in the presence of a true enthusiast.

On no account should you confuse him with Maurice Schumann, a one-time Minister, better known for being the French voice of BBC London during 1940-44.

Should you ever run into someone you suspect of being a fellow bluffer you might try pricking his pretensions with the question: "Which Schuman(n) do you mean – Robert or Maurice?"

Paul-Henri Spaak (1899-1982)

Paul-Henri Spaak is a useful name to remember if ever you find yourself playing the game 'Five Famous Belgians', which involves naming five citizens of that land anybody's ever heard of. It's virtually impossible unless you cheat (King Leopold I, King Leopold II, ...).

But it did produce Paul-Henri a distinguished fellow

who was his country's first Socialist Prime Minister, (1938-39), and who spent the war in exile in London, rallying the anti-Nazis.

His enduring claim to fame in European terms is that he was Chairman of the committee set up by the Messina Conference to draft the Treaty of Rome. So if you think the Treaty is appalling, he's one of the chaps to blame.

Altiero Spinelli (1907-1986)

Altiero Spinelli is often described as the prophet of Europe, and the title could not be more apt. His was an extraordinary vision.

A sworn enemy of Mussolini, Spinelli was seized by the fascists and confined to the island of Ventotene. While there, with the whole of Europe collapsing into darkness around him, he drew up a federalist manifesto for a United States of Europe – a dream which he hoped would be realised in happier days.

After serving in the European Commission and then the European Parliament, Spinelli died without ever seeing the realisation of that dream. Yet his work in producing the draft Treaty on European Union was vital in preparing the ground for the Single European Act. And that in turn takes Europe a long way along the road towards Spinelli's original vision.

Margaret Thatcher (1925)

Few leaders have done so much to promote unity in Europe as Mrs Thatcher: the other nations are unanimous in loathing her. Mostly their view is inspired by jealousy. Mrs. Thatcher was the only head of government in the Community who carried any clout in the world. The others found that impossible to forgive.

Their detestation was partly to do with the way she started thumping the Community table as soon as she was elected in 1979, complaining that Britain was paying too much into the European budget. The French went potty. The Germans were disdainful. The lady was accused of being a shrew, a muddled housewife, a fanatic, a crone, a witch and a chauvinist. Mrs. Thatcher didn't care. "Pooh!" she said. "It's our money!"

After two ferocious European summit rows in Dublin (1979) and Luxembourg (1980) she got her way, leaving male leaders of the EC bruised, battered and resentful. She is worth including in any list of great Euro characters, if only because her name can be guaranteed to turn any genuine European enthusiast puce with rage.

Jacques Delors (1927)

As President of the Commission, Frère Jacques always terrified his fellow Eurocrats. He was easily the most formidable boss the Commission ever had. Even on his holidays he read books on European history and politics. He was the truest of true believers.

Without Delors' vision and drive, it is unlikely that there would ever have been a Single European Act or the Maastricht Treaties. If you hate the way Europe is developing into a superstate, the villain who should earn most of your hisses is undoubtedly Jacques the lad.

CITIES OF THE UNION

Nothing will better establish your reputation as an expert in all things European than a sound working knowledge of the key cities in the Union.

Mention Strasbourg to a real Eurobuff and as likely as not he'll roll his eyes in ecstasy and exclaim: "Ah, the onion tarts! The asparagus!" Talk of Brussels and he'll drool over the restaurants around the Grand 'Place. As for Luxembourg, every expert knows that there is hardly a better place anywhere for living it up on the cheap.

Fortunately the bluffer need only concern himself with these three cities. Places like London, Paris Amsterdam and Madrid have no regular function in the life of the EU, except as places where Euro MPs and Eurocrats sometimes go for a discreet dirty weekend.

Luxembourg

Luxembourg is one of those oddities of Europe's turbulent history, a Grand Duchy which has somehow managed to maintain its independence against all the odds. Straddling the motorway between Brussels and Strasbourg it is so small that you can miss it altogether if you blink.

The only thing most people know about Luxembourg is that it had Europe's most venerable pop radio station, which once broadcast the adventures of the great spaceman Dan Dare as he fought the evil Mekon.

In fact, the Grand Duchy has one great distinction. A recent survey showed that it has the world's highest per capita consumption of alcohol and cigarettes. However you should not be misled into believing that its people are enjoying a long, riotous binge. The survey result owes everything to the fact that people passing through the country all load up with cheap booze and tobacco.

The Grand Duchy's low taxes mean that everyone who lives there is coining a fortune from tourists. Low taxes also explain why Eurocrats, mainly from the European Parliament, have to be dragged kicking and screaming across the frontier when they are relocated in Brussels – a fate which is being inflicted on them more and more frequently.

No wonder they object to moving. Not only do EU employees in Luxembourg enjoy low taxes, cheap drinks and cheap smokes, but they are also entitled to a new car, entirely free of tax, every eighteen months.

All in all, it seems a shame that Luxembourg never became the capital of Europe. It might easily have happened, but for a canny local bishop and an architectural blunder. Years ago, when the EEC was getting into its stride, the Grand Duchy seemed set to become the Community capital until it dawned on the bishop that the influx of foreigners meant the true-born Luxembourgeoise would soon be outnumbered. The Reverend gentleman wasn't having that if he could help it. Nobody knows what prayers the bishop offered up to save the Grand Duchy from its fate. Whatever they were, they obviously worked.

As part of its bid to become Europe's capital, Luxembourg built a modernistic parliament, a construction designed to hang daringly over the motorway. Legend says that no sooner was it built than the experts decreed it was in danger of collapse. That was the end of the dream. Unwilling to risk the lives of precious Euro MPs, the authorities decided that the Parliament should go to Strasbourg instead.

Nowadays only a few diehard technical staff occupy the forlorn-looking European Centre, which stands high on a pine-clad hill overlooking the ancient city.

Today Luxembourg is a bit of a backwater in EU terms, though the European Court of Justice sits there and a few Parliamentary committees meet there from time to time.

Don't let that fact put you off. You can earn plenty of points by claiming to know the place. And it is useful to know that visiting Eurocrats can usually be found in one of the excellent restaurants in the area. Try dropping the names of The Grunewald (just outside town) best known for its traditional food, and The Michel also on the outskirts, noted for its nouvelle cuisine.

Many bon viveurs just pop across to France for a meal, and bluffers may refer knowledgeably to the Relais du Château, at Menderen.

Strasbourg

Strasbourg is the capital of Alsace, and is one of those towns which used to be grabbed with monotonous regularity by the Germans and just as monotonously restored to the French. To this day it remains a strange blend of teutonic sombreness and French gaiety.

The idea of locating the European Parliament there, in the excruciatingly ugly Palais de l'Europe, is that it would symbolise Franco-German* reconciliation.

This is the kind of stuff which the genuine enthusi-

* Note the implied assumption that only France and Germany really matter in EU terms. This may be true. But it is a little tactless of both countries to be so obvious about it.

ast comes out with all the time. Don't be taken in. Whatever the original reason may have been for choosing Strasbourg you may cheerfully assert that nowadays the only reason the European Parliament remains in the town is because of the near-frantic efforts of the locals to keep it there.

It is little wonder that they are so fearful the Euro MPs will desert them for the convenience of Brussels. Though the full Parliament sits for just one week in every month, the MEPs and officials spend something approaching £150 millions every year in the town, browsing, sluicing and having a good time.

Certainly hotel rooms are at a premium whenever the Parliament meets, and the wise bluffer will never turn up without a firm booking. Bars, bistros, restaurants, shops, taxi-drivers and ladies of the night all share in the bonanza.

The good citizens of Strasbourg of course fiercely deny that they are dependent on the high-rolling Parliamentarians. Maybe they aren't. But Euro MPs certainly provide the jam in the doughnut. Why else would the Mayor of Strasbourg go to the trouble of erecting a huge marquee every year, to entertain the entire Parliament to a feast of the local delicacy, white Alsace asparagus?

Be sure to mention the marvellous meals you can eat at The Crocodile, the most exclusive restaurant in town. This is where heads of government and prime ministers tend to congregate. It is also the spot where a British MEP and a Parliamentary official once notoriously ate and drank their way through a gargantuan dinner, which set the pair of them back £400.

Ministers are generally entertained at the Orangerie in the park across the road from the Council buildings. But if you really want to demonstrate that you're in the know, drop in at the tiny atmospheric L'Orangerie in the Allée de la Robertsau. This is where Euro MPs, officials and journalists gather regularly, to complain about what a hard life they're having.

Or grab a table at the Maison du Boeuf on the edge of Petty France, where the idea for this Guide was born during a late and very convivial dinner.

Brussels

Brussels is a schizophrenic city. It is even spelt three ways. The local French speakers (who look down on the Flemish) call it Bruxelles. The Flemings (who hate the French) call it Brussel. Everybody else spells it with an 's' on the end.

To the Germans it has always been a convenient stopover for their troops to let their hair down on their way to sort out the French. Wellington and his men had a ball there on the eve of the Battle of Waterloo, which took place at the small hamlet just on the outskirts.

Like most other folk, the Belgians hate the Eurocrats and the sprawling buildings which house the institutions of the EU. The fact that Brussels is the de facto capital of the Union is small consolation for the way so many historic streets and fine pieces of architecture have been torn up to make way for the concrete and glass monstrosities which make up the headquarters of the Union.

The dilapidated Berlaymont still dominates the skyline of Euro-land, though the Commission long ago moved out to a building of almost equal ugliness, the sandy-coloured Breydel. MEPs inhabit l'Espace Leopold, often described as the world's tallest greenhouse.

The great thing about Brussels is that it is an easy

city to get away from. But whatever you do, don't make the mistake of saying so to a Belgian, because they retain a great pride in their capital, in spite of everything. Still, it is a fact that Eurocrats spend an inordinate amount of time planning their next holiday, or weekend in the country.

The other advantage of Brussels for the genuine European is its growing reputation as a centre of gastronomic excellence. There is no nonsense here about cuisine minceur. The Belgians have managed to retain the best traditions of French cooking, together with the quantity which has always been demanded by Flemish trenchermen.

The result is piles of good food, and chips with everything. But be warned. You need to be on Europay if the bill is not to give you indigestion.

If you want to try a truly ambitious bluff, by all means talk about the famed Maison du Cygne in the 'Grand Place, where the really top brass of the EU spend much of their time. To eat there is a rich experience, and you have to be rich to do it.

More in the sensible bluffer's line is the Atelier in the Rue Archimede, just a stone's throw from the Commission building and a regular haunt of journalists, middle-ranking officials and occasionally the odd junior Minister anxious to be spotted by reporters. Visiting lobbyists, MEPs and delegations generally stay at the Europa Hotel, just a step away from the Commission Building. Many a plot has been hatched in its intimate bar, a favourite spot for journalists meeting MEPs.

Wherever you go in Brussels, take the greatest care where you put your feet. Nobody knows why, but the city is the dog turd capital of the world, and many are the unwary who have been caught out.

POLITICAL PARTIES

The quickest way of spotting another bluffer is to raise the question of political attitudes within the European Parliament. If anyone in the room professes to know what they are, you will know at once that you have trapped a phoney.

The point is that there are 95 recognised political parties in Europe ranging from neo-Nazis to revolutionary Trotskyists, from rabid royalists to red republicans. More than 70 of those parties are represented in the European Parliament, which means that the place is a squabbling cockpit of competing ideologies. Anyone who claims to be able to make head or tail of it is either a mighty fibber, or an MEP.

This motley collection of representatives includes former priests, former strippers, former bureaucrats, old-timers batting out their fading years, newcomers hoping to make a name for themselves, enthusiasts for the European ideal, sceptics, cynics, scholars, buffoons and quite a lot of ordinary people trying to do their best. When they are not globetrotting on 'delegations,' making study tours of the world's holiday resorts or searching desperately for the location of their own constituencies, they come together at Strasbourg in a variety of alliances.

The Right

The European Right covers a multitude of sins and few of its members can ever agree on anything.

The most prominent alliance is the Christian Democrats, a group notable neither for its Democratic instincts nor its Christian virtues. It is mainly made

47

up of Germans but nowadays includes groups like the British Tories and Spain's Alianza Popular. All such parties share the same theories of government and therefore should feel comfortable working with each other. They don't. The Germans don't trust the Spanish, the Spanish don't trust the Danes, the Danes don't trust the Belgians and the Belgians don't trust the British. The British don't trust anybody. Not even each other.

The problems on the Right have not been helped by the arrival of the fiercely anti-single market and anti-GATT Europe of Nations Party, led at Strasbourg by the ebullient Jimmy Goldsmith.

Then there are the European Liberals, who despite their name are about as liberal as Attila the Hun and must be counted as part of the Right. As indeed must the group of fascists from Italy, France and Belgium who can no longer be treated simply as an embarrassing irrelevance.

The Left

The most significant group on the Left is made up of the European Socialists, now dominated by the British Labour Party. Some members of the Group are dedicated to the proposition that Europe should be turned into a collection of workers' states. Others are devoted friends of the capitalist system and have nothing to do with workers, except those they employ as butlers.

Some British Labour MEPs are convinced of the need for European unity. Others think the whole Community is a gigantic confidence trick and work feverishly to destroy it from within. Neither group trusts the other.

Another important grouping on the Left is made up of Communists. Alas the Communist influence on the

Parliament is not impressive; none of them can agree on anything. Italian Communists are pro Europe. French Communists are dubious. The Greeks are split down the middle.

After the ignominious collapse of the Soviet empire, you might expect the Communists to look somewhat shifty and avoid drawing attention to themselves.Not a bit of it. They're winning elections in Poland and Hungary. At Strasbourg, they're virtually part of the European establishment.

The Others

The Gaullists (who call themselves the European Democratic Alliance) really ought to be considered as part of the European Right but for one problem: the Irish Republicans are members, along with a couple of Greek nationalists and three Portuguese. Some of these MEPs would rather salute the Union Jack than have anything to do with the right wing. So out of deference to them, the Gaullists should be regarded as independents.

The Greens are genuinely independent, if only because none of the other parties wants anything to do with them. They are a well-meaning bunch however, and it is unfortunate that so many of their Parliamentary colleagues regard them as a nuisance. Mostly they come from Germany, Belgium and Holland, countries where saving the whale and worrying about acid rain have always attracted political support.

Lastly there is the Reverend Ian Paisley, who has a loud enough voice to be regarded as a party on his own, and he has never agreed with anyone.

1992 AND ALL THAT

Believe it or not, there are heavyweight European politicians, especially in Britain, who dream of being able to buy a toaster in Manchester, hop on a plane, and plug the same toaster into a wall-socket in Milan.

When the Single European Act was signed this seemed a grand idea. By the end of 1992* the aim was to have one giant domestic market covering all nations of the Community with similar standards, similar taxes, similar safety regulations. Heady Stuff. Any bluffer could, and frequently did, have a whale of a time explaining how the Single Market involved:

– Tax harmonisation

– Health regulation

– The abolition of duty-free allowances

– The abolition of passport controls

– The removal of educational differences

– The removal of all barriers to business.

– The harmonisation of consumer protection

– Europe-wide services in banking, insurance and transport.

No skilled bluffer will be put off for a moment by the apparent tedium of this list. Every item offers scope with which to make quite an impression. Only a little

---

* In theory these things should have been up and running by January 1st, 1993, though the competent bluffer knows perfectly well that in Europe schedules are made to be broken.

effort is required to scare the pants off any audience. Take tax harmonisation, which if you play your cards right you can use as a springboard for a whole series of emotive questions such as:

- Will VAT be imposed on food, fuel, children's clothes and newspapers? Or will those countries which already have such taxes remove them?

- Will alcohol and cigarette taxes come down? If not, why not? And what about cider?

Then refer them to:

The Maastricht Treaties

Always refer to the Maastricht Treaties in the plural. Everybody, including the Commission, gets it wrong so this will mark you out as a real expert. Or a pedant.

Signed by the Twelve in February 1992, the Treaties (on Political Union and Economic and Monetary Union) were intended to mark the most ambitious leap forward taken by the Community since it was founded. The scope was breathtaking. There would be a single European currency. A single European central bank. Common economic policies. The beginnings of a single European Government.

No wonder Eurofanatics first greeted the proposal with little yelps of delight. At one bound Europe seemed to be about to break free of its competitive nationalisms and set itself on the road to a superstate.

Oh dear.

Even before dastardly Danes temporarily wrecked the whole enterprise in their referendum, it was beginning to dawn on Europe that Maastricht was not all it

51

was cracked up to be. Britain would not accept the 'Social Chapter' (on the grounds that it molly-coddled the working classes and gave them ideas above their station). The French started fretting about their sovereignty. The Italians began worrying that they had been sold a pup. And the Germans were already whingeing about the cost.

You need not be shy in claiming that far from 'deepening' into a centrally-controlled superstate, the Community now seems more likely to go for 'widening', with many more countries joining and real power remaining in the hands of national governments.

This, however, should not stop you worrying aloud about:

The Democratic Deficit

The mere use of the term 'democratic deficit' will establish you at once as an insider, so you should drop it into the conversation at the first opportunity. What it means is that the bureaucracy in Brussels still wields huge powers while elected politicians suck their thumbs on the sidelines.

It would be nice to think that the European Parliament could step into the breach with its new powers under Maastricht. But it still seems incapable of doing much more than deciding when to break for lunch.

Things have got to such a state that Jacques Delors was tactless enough to boast: "One day national parliaments will wake up to what is happening. There will be a shock reaction, and this will create problems...."

You can say that again, Jacques.

FACING THE EXPERTS

It is the moment all bluffers dread. There you are, in full flow, sounding learned, witty and intelligent, when it dawns on you that someone in the audience is not clinging to your every word. Worse still, the wretch shows every sign of just waiting for you to finish before demolishing you in a few crushing sentences.

You are in the presence of a real expert; someone who knows what the Schengen Group is, or who understands commitology. In a moment you will surely be exposed.

Do not panic. Take a deep breath. Remind yourself that the genuine expert falls into one of three categories:

- The official who has spent years working in one of the EU institutions

- The political figure who knows all about the European Parliament

- The lobbyist or consultant.

All of them are formidable. But all have their weaknesses which may be exploited.

The Official

It is a racing certainty that any official you come across is a Eurofanatic. Like all of his kind, he is susceptible to flattery. Lay it on with a trowel.

Drop in remarks like: "Of course it's amazing how the European institutions cope at all, when you consider that the number of executives they employ is fewer than 5,000." Follow this with a winning smile and the revelation that "The Union only employs 19,000 people altogether, and that includes the doormen."

If you can cap this revelation with the comment: "The cost of the EU's offices is only £20 million" you will have done more than establish your own credentials. You will have persuaded any European official present that you are on his side.

But it may not be as simple as that. Your challenger may not be an official at all, but another breed of expert entirely, namely:

The Politician

Politicians include not only members of the European Parliament but journalists, pundits and assorted hangers-on. They know much less than the officials, but are adept at concealing their ignorance with strings of declarations, assertions and predictions. You will not defeat them easily: they were in the business of bluffing before you had woken up to the existence of the Common Market.

Against such competition, your best bet is to hurl a few facts into the discussion, and hope for the best. Try any or all of the following:

- The European Parliament costs just a fifth of the EU budget.

- Half the total cost of the Parliament represents the need to translate everything into nine official languages.

- The numbers of employees, from the Secretary-General to the part-time cleaners add up to a startling 6,000. And as new countries join the Union, the Parliament will hire even more staff.

If you can combine such comments with the assertion that MEPs are a much misunderstood bunch, whose expenses are nowhere near as vast as some folk think, you should win any politician in the company over to your side. Your only possible remaining challenger is then:

The Consultant

Consultants and lobbyists are to be found in all the capitals of Europe. Most of them are bluffers. The difference between them (or most of them) and you is that they are being paid for it.

Leave them alone. Treat them kindly. They are only trying to earn a crust.

But if ever any of them seeks to trip you up you need show no mercy. Learn the glossary in this guide and you should be able to stand up to the most determined attack. As a matter of fact if you study these pages thoroughly there is no reason at all why you should not become a lobbyist or a consultant yourself.

GLOSSARY

Eurocrats have invented a whole new language of their own. The would-be expert may be assured of his or her ability to mystify the unqualified by skillful and accurate use of this new terminology.

Accession Treaties – The membership contracts for the Community which mean that you're in, whether you like it or not.

Agricultural Guidance and Guarantee Fund – The method by which Europe's taxpayers finance the Common Agricultural Policy. A device by which the Public pays Europe's farmers to produce food which is then put into storage, destroyed, or sold to the Russians for about fourpence a ton.

Article 100 – The section of the Treaty of Rome under which Brussels can tell democratically-elected national Parliaments what to do, whether they like it or not.

Beethoven's Ninth Symphony – The last movement (a choral setting to Schiller's *Ode to Joy*) has become the European anthem. The tune is all right, but the words are a bit feeble. If you really want to show off, just quote "Alle Menschen werden Brüder', which translates roughly as "let's be pals".

BC NET (Business Co-operation Network) – An attempt to make the Community and the Single Market relevant to small businesses by encouraging them to co-operate. The programme is a disaster: businessmen would rather cut each other's throats.

BEUC (Bureau European des Unions de Consomma-
teurs) – The European Bureau of Consumers'
Unions.

Cassis de Dijon – An exotic French aperitif. Also the
name given to an important European Court case
which says that any product made in a member
state must be admitted to all the others.

CENELEC (European Committee for Electrotechnical
Standardisation) – A costly body which in spite of
propaganda has not yet overcome the fact that Britain
has plugs with three pins and everywhere else has
two.

The Channel Tunnel – Though far and away the
biggest engineering project ever undertaken in
Europe by the private sector, beware of claiming
that this is a triumph of European cooperation. To
be sure, the French are taking it very seriously
indeed, with new motorways serving the Channel
ports, the building of a special railway line from
Paris to the Tunnel and high-speed trains which will
zoom to and fro at 168 mph.

   But on the British side there are lingering doubts
about the wisdom of the scheme. Proud insularity
dies hard. Some folks worry about the threat to the
nation's island defences; others that packs of rabid
dogs might pour through to inflict a reign of terror
on Southern counties. Perhaps it is in response to
such visceral emotions that British Rail stoutly
refuses to excite itself over this new-fangled madness. There will be no special tracks to serve the
Tunnel link, at least for years to come. There will
probably be leaves on the line as well.

Commitology – Not to be confused with codology, or the study of comets, but a near-mystical understanding of how all the committees in Brussels actually take their decisions – an understanding which is not easy to achieve since the process of decision-taking varies so much from committee to committee. Do not play bluffers' games with anyone who understands Commitology. You will be eaten alive.

Competing products – A term covering the endless cock-ups which occur when the Brussels bureaucrats try to tax one product in excess supply, only to find that they have encouraged another. A classic case was the attempt to tax butter, which ended in the entire Continent being buried in margarine.

Competition Policy – A wide-ranging term covering mergers and state aid to industry, which means that no nation state is allowed to compete with another.

Consultative document – Bumf sent out by the Commission to advisory bodies, whose opinions it then ignores.

Co-responsibility levy – A tax on excess production which makes farmers pay towards the cost of disposal of the crops which Brussels encouraged them to grow in the first place.

Derogation – A temporary let-off from obeying some piece of Euro lunacy.

Directive – An order from the Community to a member state to implement some piece of madness. Or else.

Ecu – The single European currency to which everyone but Britain is committed. The idea is that all the currencies of Europe (Pound, Mark, Franc) should have a common Ecu value – that is, if Britain joins in and the others don't drop out.

EFTA (European Free Trade Area) – A bunch of no-hopers, who have now given up and applied to join the Union.

EMS – European Monetary System set up in 1979 to align currency rates. It was intended as the first step towards the creation of **EMU** (Economic and Monetary Union). It proved a disaster for Britain. In the attempt to maintain the pound's value within the **ERM** (Exchange-Rate Mechanism), interest rates were kept dangerously high. Thousands of businesses went bust. Thus on 'Black Wednesday' (16 September 1992), Britain was forced to leave the ERM. Its economy has been growing faster than any other country in Europe ever since.

ERASMUS – A programme for the exchange of university students between the member states. Named after the great 17th century humanist from Rotterdam.

ERGO – European Community Action Programme for the Unemployed. Since it was set up, unemployment hasn't stopped rising.

European Court of Human Rights – Nothing to do with the EU or the Court of Justice in Luxembourg, but the splendid body which banned the flogging of naughty boys in British schools. It is regarded with great suspicion by those who were beaten endlessly in their schooldays and are convinced it never did them any harm.

European Space Agency – Agency founded in 1975 which aims to promote the peaceful application of space research and technology. In practical terms, the French build the rockets while the rest of Europe pays them to do it.

European Investment Bank – An independent institution set up under the Treaty of Rome with the aim of contributing to the balanced development of the Union. It grants long-term loans and guarantees to public authorities and financial institutions to finance investment favouring less prosperous regions.

Eurovision Song Contest – One of the very few man-made disasters in today's Europe which has nothing to do with the EU.

Fifth Freedom – A splendid bit of Euro pomposity covering the right of an airline to fly from one country to another, collecting passengers.

GSP – Generalised System of Preference, allowing developing countries reduced tariffs on their exports to the EU.

HDTV (High Definition Television) – A French plot to help their industries capture the television market with an allegedly better system which would be foisted on the rest of the EU. So far unsuccessful thanks to opposition from satellite TV and the abysmal standard of French programmes.

LINGUA – A programme to promote the learning of foreign languages throughout the EU. Largely unnecessary, since everybody is already learning English.

Luxembourg Compromise – The deal which settled the Community's worst-ever political crisis when France disrupted business for seven months by adopting an 'empty chair' policy at European meetings. Member states agreed that the Council of Ministers should attempt to reach unanimous decisions in areas where any member claims a vital national interest to be at stake. In short, the Luxembourg Compromise preserved a limited veto. Though officially scrapped at Maastricht, no-one is too clear whether it really is extinct.

Non-tariff barriers – Technical barriers to trade, such as differences in national laws, or sheer bloody mindedness.

PHARE – Programme for providing Poland, Hungary, the Czech Republic and Slovakia with economic assistance.

Plenary Session – A meeting of the whole European Parliament, usually held in Strasbourg.

Rapporteur – A Member of the European Parliament appointed to co-ordinate discussion and to write a report. Which nobody will read.

Recommendation – Commission view on European policy which nobody needs to take seriously.

Regime – Nothing to do with coups d'état, but rules worked out for individual commodity markets under the CAP. Hence the 'Sheepmeat regime'.

Schengen Group – An alliance of nine of the fifteen member states who are dedicated to tearing down the frontiers between themselves, and replacing border checks and customs officials with computer terminals and terminal queues.

Subsidiarity – A term that derives from Catholic social teaching and originally meant that the faithful should run their own show so long as they did not contradict Vatican policy. Though the idea has been adopted by the Commission, the principle has not changed. This means that things best done at national or regional level should not be subject to interference from Brussels. But since Brussels still makes the rules, the notion that nations or regions can exercise genuine independence is a bit of a bluff in itself.

Two speed Europe – The threat that the Schengen group of countries will gallop towards integration on their own, leaving the non-fanatical nations like Britain trailing miserably behind.

THE AUTHORS

Michael Toner was seduced by the European Ideal many years ago when he visited an elderly farmer in Ireland.

The old gentleman had just received a large cheque from Common Market funds, intended to finance the rebuilding of the drystone walls around his farm.

"But you haven't got any drystone walls," protested the hapless Toner. The old boy tapped the side of his nose. "Right enough," he said. "But they don't know that in Brussels."

After many years as political editor for a national Sunday newspaper, Michael Toner is now a freelance journalist. He lives in the Northern home counties with his wife Carol, endless children, a cat and a hamster. He is currently engaged in drafting an application to Brussels for finance to rebuild his drystone wall.

Christopher White is our mole inside the European Institutions. After many years in Fleet Street he joined the Brussels gravy train and spent five years continuing a Fleet Street tradition of dining out in a style that the bureaucrats think they invented. He says he got the job as a press officer in the European Parliament after a long lunch.

He lives in Brussels with his wife Anne and son Nicholas, but has now left the European Parliament to work as a freelance journalist and broadcaster because he feels that the fun is going out of being a bureaucrat since the responsibilities of telling people what to do have begun to impinge on the lunch hours.

THE BLUFFER'S GUIDES®

Available at £1.99* and £2.50 each:

Accountancy

Advertising

Antiques*

Archaeology

Astrology & Fortune Telling*

Ballet*

Bluffing

British Class*

Champagne

Chess

The Classics

Computers

Consultancy

Cricket

Doctoring

Economics

The European Union

Finance

The Flight Deck

Golf

The Internet

Jazz

Journalism*

Law

Literature*

Management

Marketing

Maths*

Modern Art

Music

The Occult*

Opera

Paris

Philosophy

Photography*

Poetry*

P.R.

Public Speaking

Publishing*

The Quantum Universe

The Races

The Rock Music Business

Rugby

Science

Secretaries

Seduction

Sex

Skiing

Small Business

Teaching

Theatre*

University

Whisky

Wine

All these books are available at your local bookshop or newsagent, or by post or telephone from: B.B.C.S., P.O.Box 941, Hull HU1 3VQ. (24 hour Telephone Credit Card Line: 01482 224626)

Please add the following for postage charges: UK (& BFPO) Orders: £1.00 for the first book & 50p for each additional book up to a maximum of £2.50; Overseas (& Eire) Orders: £2.00 for the first book, £1.00 for the second & 50p for each additional book.